MANIFESTATION JOURNAL FOR BEGINNERS

An Introduction to Harnessing
the Law of Attraction
&
Journal for Creating the
Life You Want

LAURI ALBERT

ROCKRIDGE
PRESS

Interior and Cover Designer: Helen Bruno
Art Producer: Sara Feinstein
Editor: Nora Spiegel
Production Editor: Jax Berman
Production Manager: Riley Hoffman

Illustration used under license from Creative Market.

Paperback ISBN: 978-1-63807-372-7
eBook ISBN: 978-1-63878-276-6
R0

TO KEITH

Thank you for always supporting me.
I'm so grateful I manifested you!

*"There are no limits to
what you can create for
you, because your ability
to think is unlimited!"*

—RHONDA BYRNE

Contents

INTRODUCTION   vi

HOW TO USE THIS BOOK   viii

PART ONE: A Beginner's Guide to Manifestation   1

CHAPTER ONE: Manifesting 101   3

CHAPTER TWO: The Law of Attraction   15

CHAPTER THREE: Manifesting through Journaling   25

PART TWO: Your Manifestation Journal   37

A FINAL WORD   91

RESOURCES   92

REFERENCES   93

Introduction

I AM SO EXCITED YOU PICKED up this book! Just the fact that you did so means you are ready to take steps to enhance your life and create lasting joy. Please know that *you* are the only one who can really do that! This is a journey that will see you smile, laugh, cry, go deep, and realize things about yourself you have never considered before. Doesn't that sound exhilarating?

I am a spiritual medium, meditation teacher, podcast host, and empowerment coach. Throughout my life, I've studied the philosophies of many spiritual teachers and gurus. At one point, I realized that, regardless of their religion or ideology, all these teachers seemed to have at least one belief in common: Living in the present moment is where true joy rests. This realization set me on a path of incredible self-discovery and down a road I never dreamed I would explore. I learned about the universal laws and how to manifest the most unbelievably amazing life. Now, I have the enormous honor of passing on some of the wisdom I've acquired. This book is a manifestation of mine and channeled by my Spirit guides for you! How cool is that?

The idea of manifesting the life we wish to lead is quite simple. We get to use the incredible power of our thoughts to dive into our deepest desires and, ultimately, create our dream life! However, it *is* a commitment; manifestation requires work—fun work, but, yes, work. As we live our lives, it can be easy to just go with the flow, pushing our dreams and goals further and further to the side until we lose sight of them. Manifestation empowers us and gives us the freedom to dream and use the words, "What if?" This process can be challenging for some people, but just making the choice to do this work and devoting yourself to the process is an essential first step.

Manifestation work teaches us to be grateful for what we have, to feel confidence in our lives right now, to raise our personal vibration, and so much more. It's about making the choice and beginning to visualize a reality in which we feel peace, satisfaction, and bliss. The Law of Attraction comes into play with manifesting in a significant way. This universal law states that "like attracts like." Our thoughts are energy, so if we think positively and put out positive energy, we attract positive energy. *This* is where the importance of the ideas in this book come into play.

Self-help author Bob Proctor said, "Thoughts become things. If you see it in your mind, you will hold it in your hand." This quote rocked my world the first time I heard it, and I remember thinking, *Is this really possible?* Then, the 2006 movie *The Secret* came out, followed by the book *The Secret* by Rhonda Byrne, which brought it all home for me. As both the movie and book explain, there is tremendous power in our thoughts. Since that time, my life has never been the same.

As you begin this journey, my promise to you is this: If you make the decision to change your life, begin to use the tools in this book, and work from your heart, you will feel happier, more satisfied, and more empowered than you've ever felt before. This work can be unbelievably insightful and uplifting, but it should not take the place of any therapy, medication, or treatment plan you may have with your doctor or other health care provider. Working with health professionals *and* doing this manifesting work at the same time is always the way to go.

The first step toward creating a life that will bring you extraordinary love and joy is committing to a daily journaling practice, which can have huge beneficial effects, as I've seen firsthand. Adopting a journaling routine as well as taking on the other practices discussed here will help you establish lifestyle changes and create new habits that will transform the way you look at your life . . . for the better! Also, remember, this process is supposed to be fun! Staying lighthearted and joyful is what helps you manifest most quickly.

How to Use This Book

BEGIN BY READING PART 1, THE "getting to know you" phase, with all the tools, definitions, and explanations surrounding manifestation, the Law of Attraction, and journaling. Take notes, dog-ear pages if you'd like, insert sticky notes, or highlight information you'd like to remember or reread. This part of the book gives you the foundation to start manifesting what you want in your life. Keep the motivational tips and guidelines in mind as you move on to the journaling exercises.

Part 2, the journal, is where you will get down to work and creation begins! If you keep your thoughts light and positive as you do the work, it won't even seem like work. You'll probably feel a gamut of emotions as you delve into this process, so go easy on yourself. Remember, Rome wasn't built in a day, but it *was* built. Remember, too, that no one is perfect. So, if you falter one day, just dust yourself off and start again the next day. The most important thing is to keep going. What's great about this journal is that you can always turn back to part one if you forget something or need a refresher.

....

A Beginner's Guide to Manifestation

In this first part, you'll begin to understand what manifestation really is, its history, and how to tailor it to fit your life. You'll also start the process of choosing what it is you want to manifest. Then, you'll learn about the vast collection of techniques that help you advance along the path of building your ultimate life. Some tools will sound exciting and easy to incorporate into your life, but others may seem somewhat challenging. The idea is to step out of your comfort zone a bit and motivate yourself to change unhealthy habits or thought processes you may have created over time.

"*You create your thoughts, your thoughts create your intentions, and your intentions create your reality.*"

—WAYNE W. DYER

CHAPTER ONE

Manifesting 101

THE IDEA OF HAVING THE LIFE of your dreams and any
thing you really want may sound pretty "pie in the sky" to
many people, but the reality is, if you really want a better,
more fulfilling life, it *can* be achieved beyond anything
you've ever considered. In this chapter, you'll learn about
manifestation and how it works. You'll also discover a
variety of manifestation techniques and how to use them
to plan your course of action to create the life you desire.

What Is Manifestation?

Manifestation is using the power of your mind and thoughts to will
anything you truly want into existence. Yes, it sounds kind of mag-
ical, but guess what? The magic is within you! Like Dorothy in *The
Wizard of Oz*, you have the power within you. With this power, you
can create incredible things . . . anything from the best parking spot
in the lot to achieving your ultimate dream job to finding the love
of your life. It's all inside you. The key is learning how to unleash
the power of managing your thoughts, staying grateful for what you
already have, and never giving up.

If you find this all a bit difficult to swallow, know that Jim Carrey,
Louise Hay, Jennifer Lopez, Conor McGregor, and Oprah Winfrey

have all publicly discussed the Law of Attraction and their use of manifesting and how it made massive differences in their lives. They all have one thing in common: They put in the work and never gave up. Deciding that you are ready to jump in with both feet and change your life to one of abundance, pure joy, and genuine satisfaction could be the easiest and the hardest thing you will ever do. But you *can* do it.

The Key Components

There are three vital components of manifestation. Each one is equally as important as the others, and they should be focused on independently *and* as a set.

1. **Create it.** This is where you get to dream and imagine the amazing things you want in your life and then narrow those dreams down so you may choose what to manifest.

2. **Live it.** Here, you focus on being present in your life, as it is now, and change negative thought patterns into those of gratitude and joy using the exercises in this book.

3. **Embrace it.** Embracing and allowing mean opening your heart and mind to receiving the incredible blessings the Universe has to give you . . . and guess what? You are worthy and deserve it all!

How Does It Work?

Successful manifestation requires that we understand what we want, why we want it, and, perhaps, why we don't have it yet. It also requires self-confidence, belief in our goals, a high personal vibration, and a willingness to explore our deepest feelings. When these qualities are in place, we are able to quiet that voice in our heads telling us we don't deserve or shouldn't have our life's desires. Then, we begin to break the negative thought cycle that we've spent so long creating and form new, positive thought patterns.

How Can Manifestation Improve Your Life?

Imagine that there were a way to limit stress, anxiety, and worry in your life. That might sound like a tall order, I know. But let's consider that it's possible to find a way to live more joyfully and satisfyingly—within ourselves, in this very moment. This concept is the basis of manifestation. Yes, manifesting "things" is fun and exciting, but to manifest anything, we must first alter our thought patterns, live more in the present moment, and find gratitude for our lives *just as they are.*

Right now, you may be thinking you picked up this book because you want to *change* your life, not continue to live the life you've been living. However, when you start to understand that right here, right now, in *this* very moment, life is pretty good, you begin to see that life happens only in the present moment. This is where gratitude exists, and tapping into its power can be life changing. Once you get good at really feeling your gratitude for the present moment, manifesting your heart's desire takes on new meaning.

Let's look at some areas of life where manifestation can help. (You'll learn the techniques soon.)

Personal and Professional Goals

Perhaps you want to manifest a supervisory position at your company. You've worked hard at your current job and are sure you would be a fantastic administrator. How can manifesting help you achieve that goal? First, be specific and define exactly what it is you want this job to entail, and then believe and live as though it's already yours (in your mind only, of course) while using one or more manifestation techniques, including journaling. Following these steps creates self-confidence, an appreciation for where you are right now in your career, and the ability to expect and receive the position when it materializes.

Relationships

Most people have probably contemplated who their soul mate is—what they look like, their personality, and what life as a couple could be like. If you've done this, can you even fathom this person being even more amazing than you've already dreamed? Visualizing and journaling about your future partner's physical features, how they dress, how they speak, and how your relationship develops can help you define what you really want in a life partner—and manifest it! If you already have a partner, you can manifest an even deeper, more passionate relationship. It's possible. The first step to your heart's desire is specifying what you want while trusting with every fiber of your being that it's on the way to you.

Finances

I could use more money. How about you? Over the years, it's been my experience that some people who are new to manifesting go right for the cash, and then, when they don't win the lottery the next day, throw out the entire idea of manifestation; this is so sad. It is a bit more challenging to manifest money than other things, solely due to the raw emotions that most of us have toward it, lack of it, and accessibility to it. My advice is to start gradually by choosing something small, like a free cup of coffee. Part of this process is realizing that we can't have everything we want the minute we want it. We must work for it!

Health and Fitness

When you apply manifesting principles to health and fitness goals, you will find yourself becoming genuinely motivated and eager to continue on your fitness or health journey. The more you work at manifesting your fitness- or health-related goals and begin to see progress, the easier it becomes to trust in the power of your thoughts to make beneficial changes in this area of your life. The excitement becomes palpable because you can see and experience results. Please note that you should *always* continue working with any health care professionals during this process.

A Very Brief History of Manifestation

As a practice, manifestation is a relatively new concept based on its association with the Law of Attraction—that "like attracts like." However, the idea of obtaining your heart's desire and achieving everything you want in life through the power of your mind goes all the way back to ancient times. For example, in chapter 6, verse 5 of the Bhagavad Gita, which was written by Vyasa sometime between 400 BCE and 200 CE, Krishna states, "Reshape yourself by the power of your will. Never let yourself be degraded by self-will. The will is the only friend of the Self, and the will is the only enemy of the Self."

In the early 19th century, the New Thought movement in the United States brought to light the ancient spiritual teachings that we are born of the Divine and, thus, have the ability, through our thoughts, to achieve anything we want in our lives. The term "Law of Attraction" was brought into play by New Thought founder Phineas Quimby when he incorporated the practice into his teachings. The belief is that "like attracts like" and what you put your mind's attention to is what comes back to you.

Most recently, manifestation and the Law of Attraction have become hugely popular in the West due to Abraham-Hicks seminars and work published by Abraham-Hicks Publications and Rhonda Byrne, the creator behind *The Secret* and the author of the book by the same title. These works, and others like them, bring to life, in real-world ways, the teachings of how to focus your attention on what you want.

A Variety of Techniques for Manifesting

Let's dive in, shall we? I love talking about all the different techniques for manifesting. There is so much we can do to lift ourselves up to a place of joy on an ongoing basis. The secret to all of these techniques is teaching ourselves how to *stay* in that place of joy, gratitude, and fulfillment. That's where these tools enter the equation.

Learning how to get creative and have fun with your imagination helps keep your mind in that place of happiness and positivity. Being in that place of happiness, in turn, keeps your vibration high, allowing you to attract all those things you want into your existence. Remember, the Law of Attraction states that like attracts like, so when we stay "upbeat and happy," we attract "upbeat and happy."

Doing one or more of the following techniques multiple times each day, along with journaling, will continually remind you to stay positive, focused, and joyful as you progress in shifting your thought patterns. As you try these techniques, you may find that you gravitate toward some and not others. Be gentle with yourself, but try them all first. Later, if you find that you would like to change things, it will help to be familiar with all your options.

Visualization

When you were young, did you daydream about being older and what you would do with your life? Most of us did. And "daydream" is what you get to do here! Set aside some time to sit still and visualize, allowing your imagination to go wild without limits. Want to ride an elephant? Sure, why not? Want to fly into space? Do it! There are no limits to what you can do in your mind! When you first start using this visualization technique, it may seem ridiculous, but the more you permit yourself to pretend the way you did when you were young, the more real and significant your thoughts become. Visualizing daily can set your mind free to explore limitless possibilities!

Vision Board

A vision board, or dream board, is a touchable display that you can continually view and let soak into your consciousness. A vision board is that concrete place where you use pictorial representations of those visualizations from your mind and create a tool to keep you focused. A poster board is a great medium on which to create a vision board. Your vision board is very personal and should be positioned in a place where you can see it often.

To create a vision board, paste or pin up pictures (and words, if you'd like) from magazines and online sites or even images you've drawn onto the board to display all your dreams and desires in one place. Your board may include words and pictures of objects, people, and activities and even images that represent emotions. It can include whatever you choose, *and* you can change it or make another one whenever you'd like.

Meditation

As a meditation teacher, I could go on forever about the benefits of this practice, but for the purposes of manifesting, sitting in stillness daily is essential to begin to transform how you see yourself, your life, and the world. Establishing a meditation practice allows you to carve out some time (even if it's just 10 minutes a day) to be still. Sometimes, while meditating, there will be "gotta do" thoughts. Gently move them to the side and simply sit and allow yourself to just be. One helpful hint to consider is that it's not necessary to sit in a certain position with your hands folded just perfectly; sit however is comfortable. As long as you do it, you are doing it correctly.

Affirmations

In the 1970s, motivational author Louise Hay popularized the practice of repeating positive affirmations to ourselves. This practice is widely used today to raise confidence, self-esteem, and self-love. A significant affirmation to start with is simply to say, "I love you" while looking into the mirror. Doing this for the first time can be jarring, and it may feel uncomfortable. However, when you repeat this phrase to yourself several times a day, you will begin to understand the positive impact it has on your self-image. From that point on, finding or creating daily positive affirmations to repeat to yourself throughout the day can become a creative game that is both fun and empowering. (The journal part of this book includes daily affirmations to get you started.)

Journaling and Scripting

Similar to visualization, in which you dream without limits, journaling and scripting are hands-on techniques for manifesting. When journaling, you write out your requests to the Universe and your positive thoughts about having them. In the process of scripting, you create written scenarios in which you already have what you are working to manifest. For instance, if what you'd like to manifest is visiting a specific country, you would write about the sights, sounds, smells, and other experiences as though you have already experienced them. Scripting regularly helps you feel what it will be like to obtain what you desire.

The journaling part of this book gives you plenty of writing space, but you may also want to have a personal journal handy to go deeper, which can be either a notebook or an electronic document if you prefer typing to writing longhand.

55x5 and 3-6-9 Methods

A compelling and relatively newer manifestation technique is referred to as the 55×5 method. To use this technique, create a sentence or two stating your desire/intention as if it has already been attained and write it 55 times every day for 5 days. With the 3-6-9 method, you write your desire as if achieved each day for 45 days: 3 times in the morning, 6 times in the afternoon, and 9 times at night. With both methods, it's important to be as detailed as possible when stating your intention and to stay extremely positive while writing to keep your vibration high.

Commit to a Consistent Practice

Now that you've learned some of the most popular techniques for manifestation, it's time to put it all together, get creative, and understand that consistency is where the treasure sits.

Establishing a very clear intention of what you are manifesting sets the tone for the entire process. The more detailed and focused the intention is, the easier it will be to visualize, which will then allow it to come into your reality sooner.

With the intention set, begin the process of paying attention and noticing your negative versus positive thoughts and emotions throughout your day. This process is an especially important part of the entire series. Catch negative thoughts and feelings the second they happen and reframe them in a positive, reaffirming light. This is where the affirmations, meditation, vision boards, and other techniques come into play. By consistently looking at your vision board, writing in your journal, scripting, meditating, and using positive affirmations multiple times a day, you purge negativity from your being and invite in contentment, gratification, and joy.

Changing your negative thought processes to ones of positivity, though, must also include embracing the outcome. You need to believe and truly grasp that you deserve every wonderful thing life brings you! With this belief at the forefront of your thoughts, commit to consistency going in, put the intentions and techniques in place, and set aside time every day, throughout the day, to do the work.

WHY CONSISTENCY IS KEY

Throughout this manifestation process, you will have fantastic days when you feel like you've tackled the unhealthy habits that prevent you from manifesting anything and transformed them into amazingly positive, high-vibrational routines. However, get ready: There will, unfortunately, also be low days when you feel defeated and as if the Universe is conspiring against you! Fear not, and remember the following:

» It takes time to build the transformation muscle. Just as you do when you exercise, you must keep up the workout routine to see results.

» You must be gentle with yourself on days when you feel disheartened. The foremost thing to remember is to keep going . . . never stop. On great days, the visualization, affirmations, journaling, and gratitude are easy, but the real work is on the low days.

» On any off day, forcing yourself to write a list of what you are grateful for *will* begin raising you back up. My motto is, "When in doubt, drop and give me five *gratefuls*." This is to say, at the very least, find gratitude every day.

» If you find yourself having more low days than high ones, it's time to rethink your manifestation process. Maybe analyze the techniques you do every day and consider modifying the time you do them or focusing on those techniques you love doing more than others. Aside from being consistent, there is no one right way to do any of this. It's all what works for you.

Manifestation Can Change Your Life

One of the extraordinary things about manifestation is its effect on our entire life—not just the physical things we wish to generate from it. The best way to manifest love, a new car, your soul mate, or simply more joy in your life is to implement the techniques and suggestions in this book. Paying attention to and recognizing pessimistic and undesirable thoughts and educating yourself on how to replace those thoughts with uplifting, positive, and optimistic ones will change your outlook on yourself, your life, and the entire world.

Once I began identifying my negative thought patterns and what triggered them, along with using the tools in this book, I was able to exchange negative thoughts for happy, uplifting ones. My continuing daily personal use of meditation, affirmations, gratitude, and visualization still puts a smile on my face, and it will for you, too.

As I shared earlier, manifestation does require work, and some of it could be emotionally challenging, but if you want your life to be surprisingly exciting, fulfilling, and joyful, this is an incredible way to accomplish that.

REFLECT ON WHERE YOU STARTED

As you continue through this journey, you may or may not realize the internal transformation that is happening to you. It's a really good idea to look back through your journal occasionally to see how far you've come and the remarkable changes occurring within. Embracing a fresh mindset can have a funny way of creating newfound peace that not only you notice, but so does everyone around you! Somehow, you become less triggered by small things and have more patience for people and situations. You happily begin to observe gratitude in unpleasant conditions and turn those moments of feeling dismayed into flashes of incredible courage.

Looking back at this moment five years from now will be a reality check as to the brand-new world you have created for yourself. As your overall energy shifts to a more high-vibrational state, you also start to realize that energy does not know age, gender, race, religion, or sexuality. We all have the ability to create better lives based on transforming our mindset.

Let's Get Started

Getting organized can help you maintain the consistency needed for overall success when manifesting. Planning the week ahead allows you to concentrate on the steps more fully.

You've probably already been considering what you would like to manifest as a first possibility with step 1: Create It. You now need to home in and consider all the details of what you desire. Think about how you feel with that thing you desire and what it looks like. Imagine how your life would be different with it. Get very clear on what "it" is. Step 2, Live It, is about organizing the techniques you will use and spacing them out so you do the work multiple times throughout the day.

Here are some ideas to get started: Maybe you begin each day with gratitude and meditation. Then, midmorning, you work on affirmations. At lunch, you write in your journal. If you are using the 55×5 or 3-6-9 method, incorporate the technique into your day per the guidelines. In the evening, maybe you work on your vision board or, perhaps, sit and visualize your life. Then, as the evening wears down, you work on scripting and list more *gratefuls*—things you are grateful for—in your journal.

Whatever daily practice you decide upon, every night before you go to bed, say thank you to the Universe for all the amazing things coming your way. This is step 3: Embrace It. Never forget that this aspect of manifestation is just as important as the first two steps.

CHAPTER TWO

The Law of Attraction

THIS CHAPTER CONNECTS THE DOTS BETWEEN mani-festation and the Law of Attraction. You'll learn about the relationship between these concepts and how we are affected by our emotional state, as well as the huge role gratitude plays in successfully manifesting the life we dream. You'll also learn the importance of paying attention to your thoughts and how to stop negative patterns in their tracks by using the power of your mind. Opening up to new ideas and philosophies invites in a new and exciting realm of possibility.

What Is the Law of Attraction?

The Law of Attraction is a philosophy that simply states that "like attracts like." This means that whatever energy we put out into the world will then attract situations and people with the same energy to us. Whether that energy is positive or negative is up to us. Here's a perfect example of "like attracts like:" You meet someone and instantly feel a connection. You may have strikingly similar beliefs and ways of living and maybe even a similar sense of humor. You feel that spark of attraction, whether it's friendship or otherwise. Guess what? You attracted that person into your life and consciousness, but how? Let's look at how the Law of Attraction works.

How Does It Work?

The law of vibration states that everything in the Universe is in motion, or vibrating with energy. This law explains that the apple we are eating is energy, the trees standing tall outside are energy, and the car we drive is energy. And more mind-blowing, *we* are energy, and this energy never stops moving, or vibrating. Every single thing we can see, touch, and think about has its very own vibration, including us, at varying frequencies.

Because like attracts like, when we vibrate peace and calm through our thoughts and actions, peace and calm are what we attract into our lives. Likewise, if we vibrate at a happy rate, we attract happy people and situations into our lives. However, by the same token, if we constantly vibrate negativity through our thoughts and actions, we attract negative things and people into our existence. That's why your thoughts and thought processes are widely featured in this book. The idea is to vibrate at the same rate as what you want to manifest, to attract it into your life. We'll delve into this more deeply as we proceed through the chapter.

The Role of the Law of Attraction in Manifestation

In terms of manifestation and creating the life of our dreams, the Law of Attraction is the philosophy used in this process of obtaining our desires. For example, if we decide we want to manifest a loving relationship, remembering that like attracts like, it is necessary for our personal energy to vibrate love. For us to vibrate love, we must keep our thoughts and thought patterns in that high vibration of love. At the same time, using the steps and tools of manifestation, our vibration is able to continually stay at this high level, which is when manifestation occurs and we accomplish our intention.

One caveat is that most of us have in place, sadly, some disruptive thought patterns that have been within us for a long, long while. These are the thoughts that tell us we don't deserve our deepest desires and, no matter how hard we try, we will never realize our goals. The need to change these disruptive patterns is why the steps and tools in the manifestation process are so valuable. Your objective is to learn to rise above and overcome those negative thoughts and replace them with a new, positive mindset.

The Principle of the Law of Attraction

There are many interpretations of the Law of Attraction—what it is, how it works, and *if* it works. But the reality is it all goes back to that one basic principle: like attracts like. If I truly believe I can create anything I want in my life, then I will. If I expect miracles to happen, they will. On the other hand, if that terrible, ugly voice in my head tells me I am not good enough to have my deepest dreams be my reality—and I believe it—I won't ever obtain what I long for.

So, the true key to manifesting literally anything you truly want is to use all the tools at your disposal to help you raise your vibration and overcome negative beliefs and thoughts. Unfortunately, some people never overcome those negative thought patterns. However, if you surrender to this manifestation process and commit to the work, your life will transform in such a way that, when you look back, you will be astounded by how far you've come! The following discussions will help you on your way.

Shift Your Mindset

At this point, you may be wondering how to stop thinking negative thoughts. This is where it gets interesting. When you begin to pay close attention to your thoughts, you start to notice your thought patterns. Take note of when you think negative things *and* what triggers them. It's a good idea to set aside a few days to make a concerted effort to observe your thoughts closely. Once you recognize your triggers, you can find affirmations and buzzwords or phrases you can say to yourself immediately to pull you out of that negative space and jolt you into a more positive outlook.

LET GO OF NEGATIVE BELIEFS

You may be aware that you have unkind thoughts toward certain situations and/or people (maybe even yourself) due to negative beliefs you may hold. Are you willing to release those negative beliefs and look at those people and/or situations in a different light? Sometimes, just shifting to a place of compassion can have a huge effect on your inner being. For example, when you randomly run into that irritating acquaintance on the street, instead of hiding out, think, *I am love* and greet them. Watch what happens next. It is truly beautiful what a little compassion for yourself and others can do.

MAKE ROOM FOR POSITIVITY

There is power in deciding to become more positive. Recognizing when your mind goes south and inserting something happy or love-centered helps you on your way to a complete mindset makeover. For example, if a potential love interest suddenly disappears, rather than dwelling on the negative aspect of being alone and criticizing them for their lack of follow-through, consider thanking the Universe that you didn't end up with them and recognize that you now have room for your dream partner to show up! In this way, changing your thoughts depends a great deal on changing your perspective from one of negativity to one of positivity.

Set Specific Goals and Intentions

What do you truly want to bring into your life? As you work on modifying your mindset into a place of positivity and gratitude, you must also fine-tune your desires and create intentions for yourself. These goals should be centered on shifting your thoughts and defining what you wish to manifest. Undertaking all of these processes simultaneously and keeping the intentions and thought exchanges at the forefront of your mind are vital components for the success of the entire process.

THE MORE SPECIFIC THE BETTER

As you hone your requests to the Universe, a great question to ask yourself, once you identify what you might want, is, "Why do I want this particular thing?" You ask why and consider the answer. Doing this multiple times and digging deep is how you find your truth. This exercise helps you gain insight into your heart and keeps you focused on your truest desires.

Raise Your Vibration

Now that you've learned that we humans are made up of energy and that this energy is continually vibrating, let's talk about ways to inspire your personal energy to stay high and in a place of joy and love. Dancing, meditating, taking a walk, watching the ocean, listening to a favorite song, counting blessings, performing an act of kindness, and so much more are amazing ways to get you out of any funk and into that higher state. Keep your list of vibration-raising options handy so, when the need arises, the tools to lift you up are close by.

REMEMBER, LIKE ATTRACTS LIKE

The point of keeping your vibration high is simple. Always keep in mind the Law of Attraction principle "like attracts like." If you are doing or thinking something, ask yourself whether you want to attract more of whatever it is. If the answer is no, refocus on vibrating at a level of joy to attract things that bring you joy. If your vibration stays at a level of worry, you will attract people and things that bring more worry. What you choose is up to you. At any point, you can always decide to raise your vibration.

Work in Tandem with the Universe

As you go through the process of determining what you want and why, as well as learning ways to raise your vibration, you start to realize you are not in this alone. The Universe has your back, and, when you surrender to it and allow your heart to open, the idea of manifesting "stuff" becomes slightly secondary. You start to comprehend that you can actually manifest pure love, true acceptance, or even genuine happiness along with material things. The Universe opens up all of that to each of us!

ASK FOR WHAT YOU WANT AND NEED

Revisiting the question "why do I want this particular thing?" is a fantastic way to understand and narrow down what you may want or feel you need in your life and why it seems important. Getting clear about why you feel such a great need for a certain house or car, for instance, allows you to go deeper into the potentially hidden reasons for your desires and enables you to express those reasons to the Universe. This is when manifesting breaks everything wide open!

NOTHING WILL CHANGE IF YOU DON'T TAKE ACTION

Earlier, I mentioned that the practice of manifestation takes some work. Here's where it gets real: Yes, to be extraordinarily successful at manifesting, you need to consider your thoughts constantly, raise your vibration, and create amazingly detailed intentions that will rock your world. Always keep in mind: If you don't work it, it won't work. But there's more. In anticipation of your intention coming into your life, you need to keep your eyes open and take action to prepare yourself physically, mentally, and spiritually for the opportunities the Universe sends your way.

FIVE WAYS TO RAISE YOUR VIBRATION

Let's talk real-world ways to raise your vibration and stay in a place of happiness, joy, and optimism. Keeping your vibration high helps you emotionally, mentally, and physically, so paying close attention to your vibration benefits you in ways you may not even realize. Keeping your vibration high is also essential to the manifesting process. The easier it is for you to stay at a high vibration, the faster and simpler it will be for you to manifest your deepest desires. Once you get into an effortless flow, manifesting becomes unforced and natural.

Here are five things to do every day to keep your vibration elevated:

1. **Meditate.** Even if only for 10 minutes, sitting in stillness and taking time for yourself invites in a special type of peace that can keep you uplifted throughout the day.

2. **Take a walk in nature.** Connecting with Mother Earth is a powerful way to lift your soul. Fresh air and a change of scenery will renew your spirit.

3. **Dance and sing.** Who hasn't blasted their favorite song in their car or on headphones? Dancing and/or singing for at least a few minutes is guaranteed to enhance your mood.

4. **Perform an act of kindness.** Even if it's simply smiling at someone, an act of kindness can quite literally uplift someone's mood and change their day as well as your own.

5. **Self-care.** Self-care is taking time solely for yourself without feeling guilty about it. A bath, gardening, reading a book, relaxing, or just napping to recharge your batteries can instantly raise your vibration to that of true happiness.

Give Thanks

In most cases, as children, the people who raised us taught us the importance of saying, "Thank you." As adults, we must keep that same principle alive throughout this manifestation process. When we learn an impactful lesson from the Universe, whether it's a good lesson or a bad one, saying, "Thank you" keeps us in a state of higher vibration and on the path of positivity and optimism. Finding the value in a bad situation can be difficult, of course, but understanding that life is filled with lessons every day that we can learn from is how we grow.

HAVE GRATITUDE EVERY DAY

One of the best and easiest ways to keep your vibration consistently high is developing a practice of gratitude. Expressing your gratitude first thing in the morning positions your day to be filled with hope and enthusiasm. You can begin a routine of considering at least five things you are grateful for every day. As your routine takes hold, you will begin to see a difference in how you relate to the world and your place in it.

There Is Power in Positive Energy

As you've learned, the law of vibration asserts that everything in this Universe—emotions, people, things, and thoughts—is made up of energy in motion. This energy vibrates at different rates. Knowing this principle, if we keep our energy positive by thinking positive thoughts, our bodies will emit this positive vibration, which then attracts positive beings and situations to us. This is the power of positive energy.

You control this power through the Law of Attraction, by drawing to you whatever you choose, as long as you continually vibrate at the rate of that which you desire. Here's a perfect example: If you want to attract a convertible into your life, thinking positive thoughts about the car; imagining sitting in it, driving it, and feeling the wind in your hair; journaling about it; and constantly keeping foremost in your thoughts how great it would feel for this car to be yours keeps you in a high-vibration state, which then attracts the convertible into your life. How do I know this? This is how I manifested my really cool Mustang convertible! Every single day as I drove to and from work in my SUV, I would roll down the windows and smile, feeling the wind rushing through my hair. It was, and still is, exhilarating!

A Consistent Journal Practice Will Help Boost Your Vibes

Journaling about our feelings is remarkably cathartic, as anyone who has kept a journal can attest. This practice alone can raise your vibration, because you are processing your feelings while journaling. We can also use a journal to write out our dreams and intentions. The manifestation journaling process is wonderful, because it gives you the ability to look back at the dreams you took time to create and be reminded of all the amazing things you've manifested as well as how far you've come, emotionally, in the process. When the practice of journaling is consistent, you will see progress over time, which will keep you motivated and on track toward that life you dream of.

Turning negative thoughts and emotions into positive ones is vital to this process. Be sure to keep an optimistic spin on everything you write in your journal, which helps not only in the moment but also when you reread what you've written. See things from the positive perspective instead of criticizing or complaining. Remain grateful, and remember that this is supposed to be fun. Be light! You are transforming your thought patterns to create new positive habits, which takes time. Staying consistent with this practice will allow you to see the results of your hard work more quickly.

Let's Dive into Journaling

In the next chapter, let's get down to work, applying the technical information you've learned to your life! If you've never kept a journal before, you are in for some fun. The best part of journaling is that you get to write, create, and be whoever you choose to be! It is a highly personal undertaking, and your authentic self gets to shine through.

A valuable note here is to allow yourself to be real in this process. Don't be afraid to lay everything out there, but be ready to work through the hard things, to find the upbeat, encouraging, positive aspects of whatever is going on in your world to stay in the highest vibration possible. Staying positive may be a difficult task if you are used to seeing the negative side of things, but forcing yourself to look at the positives of any situation is what creates the change of habit! And consider this: what do you have to lose by trying?

CHAPTER THREE

Manifesting through Journaling

OPENING OUR HEARTS TO MANIFESTATION WORK brings a type of clarity to our lives we may never have contemplated before. When our hearts are truly open, we understand deep gratitude, the importance of self-reflection, and how living in the present moment can help us feel deep, lasting peace. As you'll learn in this chapter, all that you desire is possible through journaling. In a manifestation journaling practice, acting as though we already have what we desire, writing about it in the present tense, and feeling the gratitude that comes from receiving our wishes allows our energy to soar! Let's dive in.

The Power of the Manifestation Journal

The written word is powerful. Contemplating what to write and why to write it holds influence in your mind. Taking a reserved amount of time, once or twice a day, to write in your journal allows you to go deep within your soul to be real with yourself about your innermost longings, whether they are physical things or states of being.

Journals are places where we get to be 100 percent real with no judgment by anyone other than ourselves. Manifestation journaling is no different. Writing out your deepest desires holds that same type of power. Continuing to write in your journal about the things you want to manifest, as well as rereading what you've already written, helps those desires become all that much more real . . . and *that* is the goal. What you desire needs to feel real in your body and mind.

Esther Hicks, an expert on the Law of Attraction, described it this way via the nonphysical entity Abraham who is the source for her teachings: "The main event has never been the manifestation; the main event has always been the way you feel moment by moment, because that's what life is." To manifest anything, we need to feel that it is ours in our entire being, and the most effective way to do this is through journaling.

The Many Benefits of Using a Journal for Manifesting

One significant benefit to recording your desires and thoughts in your journal is that, in doing so, as you look back at what you have written, you are able to catch yourself and learn the triggers that cause negative thought patterns. This ability is highly beneficial in helping you alter your thoughts on an ongoing basis. It also, then, helps you figure out your personal buzzwords, phrases, or quotes that can take you off that negative path and pull you back to the world of positivity and optimistic thinking.

Another major benefit to keeping a manifestation journal is the ability to plant yourself firmly in the present moment. As you write and reflect, you recognize that this moment, right here, right now, is actually perfect, and in this moment, joy, peace, and satisfaction are all readily available. This realization is one huge point of the entire process. The ability to live in the present moment is transformational, because, as we exist in this moment, we realize the past is complete and the future hasn't yet happened. Living "in the now" reminds us that everything we need we already have.

Focus Your Mind

Once you begin the process of journaling and writing out your beliefs, dreams, emotions, goals, and intentions, you will find that just the act of writing out your thoughts on physical paper helps you focus your mind in a way that leaves you a bit more resolved, inspired, and determined. You will start to understand yourself a bit better and why it is that you want what you want. This type of complete focus is incredibly valuable when you are in the creation stage of manifestation.

Get Clear on Your Goals

Getting 100 percent clear on what we want can feel overwhelming to some people. There are so many choices! One way to figure out your deepest desires is to make a list (a long one!) in your journal. As you keep writing, your thoughts will become clearer, and you will begin to narrow down what you truly wish to manifest. Magically, at a certain point, it will be like a light bulb going off, and that "aha" moment will occur. At this point, your intuition will tell you that it's right, and you have found what it is you wish to manifest.

Specify Your Intentions

As you consider your manifestation goals, also contemplate what you may want to get out of manifesting, emotionally and mentally. When you reflect on what you want to bring into your existence, getting to the emotional and mental reason you want it can be especially insightful. Again, opening up and surrendering your heart and soul to this process can lead you down various paths to true joy and gratification. Modifying your intentions accordingly can only generate a more complete satisfaction with the outcome. This is about finding true, lasting, absolute satisfaction with yourself and your life.

Show Your Gratitude

As you've learned, expressing gratitude daily for all the great things in your life helps you stay present in the here and now. Somehow, when you read what you've written in your journal, it makes it more concrete and real, which brings about unpredicted and even deeper feelings of appreciation for your life as it is—at the present moment. This unexpected benefit of journaling might catch you by surprise, but you will be forever grateful for it because of what you begin to realize about yourself, your loved ones, and your life. Gratitude can literally change everything.

Self-Reflect and Self-Discover

Teaching yourself to write out your secret thoughts and desires in your journal can spark some big-time realizations about who you are. Journaling helps you recognize what it is you truly *want* in your life, and it is an excellent tool to help you uncover your deepest feelings. Writing in your journal assists you in discovering who you really are and who you strive to be in this world. This is yet another surprising benefit of journaling that furthers your quest to change your life to one of complete fulfillment and bliss.

Record Your Journey

As you progress through this life-changing journey, be sure to add the successes and challenges, as well as new and surprising insights you may have along the way, to your journal. Being real with yourself and not holding anything back will help you later as you reflect on your growth. Realizing that this whole process is to break down your old, stale, negative habits and ways of thinking to create fresh, positive, and confident thought patterns is what will result in victorious manifestation!

BOOST YOUR JOURNALING VIBES

What do you say about kicking journaling up a notch? I have to admit I was not into journaling when I was younger; I couldn't sit still long enough to write in a journal! I always wanted to start journaling, but for some reason, I just couldn't . . . until I became an adult and did it *my* way! Now, I love the idea of taking time just for me and sitting, writing out all my deepest thoughts.

Here's what is different: When I am about to sit down to write in my journal, I light a candle, turn on ambient music, lower the lights, meditate for about five minutes, and then jump in and begin writing. It's relaxing and allows me to sit and think without distraction. Because I meditate for a few minutes before I start, I am able to access the musings of my heart on an extraordinary level.

You may wish to incorporate some of the elements of my personal journaling practice into your routine, but there are many other ways to make the experience personal to you. For example, using crystals such as quartz, which enhances intuition, can help you access that place in your soul where your most profound desires reside. Think about what you can add to your journaling process that will uplift you. This goes for *how* you journal, too. You don't have to write in full sentences if you don't want to, and you can even draw pictures if that's how you best express yourself. The bottom line is to make it yours. Get creative and do it the way that speaks to *you*.

Scripting: A Law of Attraction Journal Technique

Earlier, I briefly touched upon scripting, the process of writing out a scenario as if it has already happened. If we exist as though we already have whatever we want, manifestation happens sooner rather than later, because, remember, like attracts like. But here's a cautionary note: In the 60,000 to 80,000 thoughts we have every single day, we all have negative, lower-vibrational thoughts that slow manifestation. Again, because like attracts like, catching those thoughts and quickly reframing them to the positive is very important, and it's where scripting comes in.

As you script scenarios in which you have the thing you want, that thing becomes real in your mind. Scripting as though you have what you desire allows you to feel the excitement and joy of that thing, and as you read your journal over and over, that excited feeling stays with you longer and longer, thereby pushing out any negative or pessimistic thoughts you may have. If you haven't realized it yet, your thoughts and emotions drive the entire process of manifestation! The following are some tips to keep in mind.

Act Like You Already Have Your Dream Life

Imagine that you want to attract a job that allows you to travel to exotic locations. Write out your script but also begin to prepare yourself for this position by learning a new language, purchasing new luggage, and creating a healthier lifestyle to make traveling easier. This will keep your vibration high with anticipation. Experiencing the feelings of this new life and job are vital, and keeping your thoughts as clear and confident as possible will attract it all that much faster.

Write Your Intentions in the Present Tense

With scripting and manifesting in general, state your desires in the present tense. For example, "I enjoy this new job and visiting new places." This is a way to, sort of, trick your brain into believing it is all happening right now. This keeps the excitement alive in your mind and body. As you create more and more entries and reread them, you experience the exhilarating feelings all over again. Scripting helps you monitor your thoughts, hold them steady and upbeat, and keep your emotions in a stimulated state.

Be Specific

Be as specific as you possibly can when visualizing and scripting. When writing your entries, it is essential to experience all five senses as you envision what you desire. Consider and imagine what you taste, smell, feel, see, and hear to capture the landscape of the intention and goal that you are working toward. Sit back and allow yourself to fantasize the entire setting, using all your senses—as if you are experiencing it right now. This can be surprisingly fulfilling and invigorating.

Record Your Emotions

Allowing yourself to get real is a huge part of the manifestation process. Getting real with your wants and needs as well as your emotional and mental state as you wade through the waters of manifesting is a fundamental condition of the process. But the great news is, you are allowed to feel whatever you are feeling, and you are encouraged to do so. Writing out your true feelings is important, but this point is key: You must then also look back at your entry and consider how you can restructure your thoughts with a positive spin. Engaging in this process daily is how you break bad habits and create good new ones.

JOURNALING FAQS

How long do the journal entries need to be?
In terms of length, let your intuition tell you. The general rule of thumb is to write until you feel "complete." You must feel satisfied that you've fully expressed yourself.

What is the best time of day to journal?
Getting into the habit of journaling twice a day is optimal: once in the morning to work on what you are grateful for and to create intentions, and then again in the evening to visualize, do scripting work, and detail your feelings and emotions from the day. Evening journaling works well so you have time to process thoughts from the day.

What do I do if I miss a day?
Start again the next day with enthusiasm. Don't make yourself wrong. Everyone falters. Success happens when we pick ourselves up and continue on!

How do I start journaling?
It's a good idea to start by just allowing yourself freedom to write. You may find that meditating first helps you relax into it.

What if the intention of what I want to manifest changes? Do I have to start all over?
Your intentions will most likely change a bit, and that is okay. It's not really about starting the process all over again. It's the continuation of the awareness of your thoughts and forming new thought patterns. Remember to give yourself a break and just keep moving forward.

Scripting Helps You Write Your Dreams into Reality

Yes, scripting is about writing out and dreaming what we want and how it will come into our existence, but there's more to scripting than that. There will be milliseconds (and sometimes more) of doubt, times when we aren't sure that this whole process is working. When we manage those thoughts, however, adjusting them to be more optimistic and positive, we start to see that we are in a creation point. Even when things don't seem as though they are working, if we know, deep in our hearts, that those strange-seeming setbacks are somehow working *for* us in the process of attaining what we want, it feels a bit simpler to keep our vibration high.

Scripting helps you confront those oddly troublesome hiccups in such a way that they turn out in your favor. What may seem like a devastating blow to your intention and goal may actually be the Universe clearing the way for something new and exciting. Sometimes things need to be cleared out before the new can enter into your consciousness. Think of it like purging the old to make way for the new. Write a script that incorporates those setbacks on your path forward in a positive light.

Let's Start Journaling

As you continue going through all the steps and exercises of manifestation, including journaling, visualization, scripting, and vision boards, your overall general energy will begin to shift, and suddenly you will find yourself starting to manifest things without even realizing it. Manifestation just starts happening, and your intentions start showing up in your reality. When these things happen, journaling gets really fun!

When you find yourself manifesting that perfect parking spot everywhere you go, be sure to write about it in your journal in earnest. Write about how you giggled when you realized what you'd done. Write about the thrill and disbelief you have as well as that feeling of "holy cow! I actually just manifested this!" These thoughts and emotions written in your journal will prove to be extremely advantageous when you decide to reread previous entries on those days when nothing seems to be going right and you are just not sure about manifestation. This is how journaling becomes valuable. Noting every emotion and thought (good and bad—and working through the bad) becomes essential to the success of obtaining every goal you set.

Your Manifestation Journal

Ready to change your life? Let's do it! Following are 50 pages to start you on your manifesting journey. I've included some prompts for you to respond to daily to help you get in touch with your state of mind and to begin your journaling on a positive, high-vibrational note. Once you've responded to the prompts, feel free to pull out your personal journal and jump into the world of writing more of your thoughts and feelings, scripting, visualizing, and recording your observations about your positive and negative thoughts. Don't forget to go easy on yourself! This is just the beginning of your manifesting journey, and it's supposed to be fun. If you find yourself stressed at all, put on some music and dance it off!

> *"A man is but the product of his thoughts. What he thinks, he becomes."*
>
> —MAHATMA GANDHI

SAMPLE JOURNAL ENTRY

Date: August 9

I can, and I will.

....

Today, I am grateful for: The great night's sleep I had last night. The butterfly and hummingbirds I get to watch right outside my window every morning. My boss, who because of his trust in me, asked that I organize and produce a slideshow for an important upcoming conference.

My intention is: My intention is to plan a fun-filled, romantic trip with my partner for us to step aside from the business of everyday life and spend time focusing on ourselves and our relationship.

The script for my intention: This trip is so much fun. We are scuba diving, fishing, and sunning ourselves by the ocean. The restaurants are fantastic, and each meal is better than the last! We are reconnecting in ways that far exceed my expectations. It's like we are 20 years old and dating again! We have coffee together in the morning in a relaxed atmosphere and actually look into each other's eyes when we talk, without having to multitask to get the day started.

Actions I can take to support my intention: I will research the most romantic resorts to stay at and plan every detail of the trip, so we are busy yet relaxed. I will find hikes and historic sites for us to explore and investigate restaurants for us to try new things, because we are adventurous and love trying new foods.

Date _____

I can, and I will.

....

Today I am grateful for: _____

_____

_____

_____

_____

My intention is: _____

_____

_____

_____

_____

The script for my intention: _____

_____

_____

_____

_____

Actions I can take to support my intention: _____

_____

_____

_____

_____

I am courageous, strong, and powerful.

Today I am grateful for:

My intention is:

The script for my intention:

Actions I can take to support my intention:

Date _____

Living in the present moment is where I find peace.

....

Today I am grateful for: _____

_____

_____

_____

_____

My intention is: _____

_____

_____

_____

The script for my intention: _____

_____

_____

_____

_____

Actions I can take to support my intention: _____

_____

_____

_____

_____

Gratitude is my middle name.

Today I am grateful for: _____

My intention is: _____

The script for my intention: _____

Actions I can take to support my intention: _____

Date _____

I love me.

....

Today I am grateful for: _____

_____

_____

_____

_____

My intention is: _____

_____

_____

_____

_____

The script for my intention: _____

_____

_____

_____

_____

Actions I can take to support my intention: _____

_____

_____

_____

_____

I manifest whatever I want
easily and effortlessly.

Today I am grateful for: _____

_____

_____

_____

_____

My intention is: _____

_____

_____

_____

The script for my intention: _____

_____

_____

_____

_____

Actions I can take to support my intention: _____

_____

_____

_____

_____

Date _____

Life always works out for me.

....

Today I am grateful for: _____

_____

_____

_____

_____

My intention is: _____

_____

_____

_____

_____

The script for my intention: _____

_____

_____

_____

_____

Actions I can take to support my intention: _____

_____

_____

_____

_____

Today, I do everything with joy in my heart.

Today I am grateful for: _____

_____

_____

_____

_____

My intention is: _____

_____

_____

_____

_____

The script for my intention: _____

_____

_____

_____

_____

Actions I can take to support my intention: _____

_____

_____

_____

_____

Date _____

I am fearless.

Today I am grateful for: ....

....

....

....

My intention is: ....

....

....

....

The script for my intention: ....

....

....

....

Actions I can take to support my intention: ....

....

....

....

I feel unconditional love with every beat of my heart.

Today I am grateful for: _____

My intention is: _____

The script for my intention: _____

Actions I can take to support my intention: _____

Date _____

I give myself permission
to be the "real" me.

....

Today I am grateful for: _____

_____

_____

_____

My intention is: _____

_____

_____

_____

The script for my intention: _____

_____

_____

_____

_____

Actions I can take to support my intention: _____

_____

_____

_____

_____

Today, I declare that I am a "yes" person!

....

Today I am grateful for: _____

_____

_____

_____

My intention is: _____

_____

_____

_____

The script for my intention: _____

_____

_____

_____

Actions I can take to support my intention: _____

_____

_____

_____

Date _____

I attract positivity everywhere I go.

....

Today I am grateful for: _____

_____

_____

_____

_____

My intention is: _____

_____

_____

_____

_____

The script for my intention: _____

_____

_____

_____

_____

Actions I can take to support my intention: _____

_____

_____

_____

_____

I trust my intuition with every decision I make.

....

Today I am grateful for: _____

_____

_____

_____

My intention is: _____

_____

_____

The script for my intention: _____

_____

_____

_____

_____

Actions I can take to support my intention: _____

_____

_____

_____

_____

Date _____

I am grateful for all the
lessons I learn every day.

Today I am grateful for: _____

_____

_____

_____

My intention is: _____

_____

_____

The script for my intention: _____

_____

_____

_____

Actions I can take to support my intention: _____

_____

_____

_____

It's okay to like myself.

....

Today I am grateful for:

_____

_____

_____

_____

My intention is:

_____

_____

_____

_____

The script for my intention:

_____

_____

_____

_____

_____

Actions I can take to support my intention:

_____

_____

_____

_____

Date _____

My heart is open.

....

Today I am grateful for: _____

_____

_____

_____

_____

My intention is: _____

_____

_____

_____

_____

The script for my intention: _____

_____

_____

_____

_____

_____

Actions I can take to support my intention: _____

_____

_____

_____

_____

I am a beacon of light shining
for the whole world to see.

Today I am grateful for: _____

_____

_____

_____

My intention is: _____

_____

_____

The script for my intention: _____

_____

_____

_____

Actions I can take to support my intention: _____

_____

_____

_____

_____

Date _____

Right here, right now, I am happy and content.

....

Today I am grateful for: _____

_____

_____

_____

_____

My intention is: _____

_____

_____

_____

The script for my intention: _____

_____

_____

_____

_____

Actions I can take to support my intention: _____

_____

_____

_____

_____

Date _____

I am enough, and the Universe loves me!

....

Today I am grateful for: _____

_____

_____

_____

_____

My intention is: _____

_____

_____

_____

_____

The script for my intention: _____

_____

_____

_____

_____

Actions I can take to support my intention: _____

_____

_____

_____

_____

Date _____

My superpower is gratitude
for everything in my life.

....

Today I am grateful for: _____

_____

_____

_____

_____

My intention is: _____

_____

_____

_____

The script for my intention: _____

_____

_____

_____

_____

Actions I can take to support my intention: _____

_____

_____

_____

_____

Date _____

Knowing that life happens in this present moment keeps me motivated.

Today I am grateful for: _____

_____

_____

_____

My intention is: _____

_____

_____

_____

The script for my intention: _____

_____

_____

_____

_____

Actions I can take to support my intention: _____

_____

_____

_____

_____

Date _____

I am beautiful!

....

Today I am grateful for: _____

_____

_____

_____

_____

My intention is: _____

_____

_____

_____

_____

The script for my intention: _____

_____

_____

_____

_____

_____

Actions I can take to support my intention: _____

_____

_____

_____

_____

Date _____

I release all negative thoughts and emotions and invite in pure positivity.

....

Today I am grateful for: _____

_____

_____

_____

My intention is: _____

_____

_____

_____

The script for my intention: _____

_____

_____

_____

_____

Actions I can take to support my intention: _____

_____

_____

_____

_____

Date _____

I am abundant in every aspect of my life.

....

Today I am grateful for: ....

....

....

....

....

My intention is: ....

....

....

....

....

The script for my intention: ....

....

....

....

....

Actions I can take to support my intention: ....

....

....

....

....

I forgive myself, and I am worthy of love, joy, and prosperity.

Today I am grateful for: _____

_____

_____

_____

My intention is: _____

_____

_____

The script for my intention: _____

_____

_____

_____

Actions I can take to support my intention: _____

_____

_____

_____

_____

Date _____

Hope is where possibility lives.

....

Today I am grateful for: _____

_____

_____

_____

My intention is: _____

_____

_____

_____

The script for my intention: _____

_____

_____

_____

Actions I can take to support my intention: _____

_____

_____

_____

Every thought has the potential to become my reality. It's all up to me.

··

Today I am grateful for: _____

_____

_____

_____

My intention is: _____

_____

_____

The script for my intention: _____

_____

_____

_____

_____

Actions I can take to support my intention: _____

_____

_____

_____

_____

Date _____

Smiling is good for my health.

....

Today I am grateful for: _____

_____

_____

_____

_____

My intention is: _____

_____

_____

_____

_____

The script for my intention: _____

_____

_____

_____

_____

Actions I can take to support my intention: _____

_____

_____

_____

_____

Patience, positivity, and persistence are the three Ps for a peaceful life.

Today I am grateful for: _____

My intention is: _____

The script for my intention: _____

Actions I can take to support my intention: _____

Date _____

Today, I choose joy!

....

Today I am grateful for: _____

_____

_____

_____

My intention is: _____

_____

_____

_____

The script for my intention: _____

_____

_____

_____

Actions I can take to support my intention: _____

_____

_____

_____

Date _____

I am powerful and confident.

....

Today I am grateful for: _____

_____

_____

_____

_____

My intention is: _____

_____

_____

_____

_____

The script for my intention: _____

_____

_____

_____

_____

Actions I can take to support my intention: _____

_____

_____

_____

_____

Date _____

I see the beauty in everything around me.

Today I am grateful for: _____

_____

_____

_____

My intention is _____

_____

_____

_____

The script for my intention: _____

_____

_____

_____

Actions I can take to support my intention: _____

_____

_____

_____

Magic happens when I open my heart.

Today I am grateful for: _____

_____

_____

_____

My intention is: _____

_____

_____

_____

The script for my intention: _____

_____

_____

_____

Actions I can take to support my intention: _____

_____

_____

_____

_____

Date _____

The Universe has my back at all times.

....

Today I am grateful for: _____

_____

_____

_____

My intention is: _____

_____

_____

_____

The script for my intention: _____

_____

_____

_____

Actions I can take to support my intention: _____

_____

_____

_____

Date _____

I believe in the power of love.

....

Today I am grateful for: _____

_____

_____

_____

_____

My intention is: _____

_____

_____

_____

The script for my intention: _____

_____

_____

_____

_____

Actions I can take to support my intention: _____

_____

_____

_____

_____

Date _____

I am thankful for everything and everyone in my life.

....

Today I am grateful for: _____

_____

_____

_____

My intention is: _____

_____

_____

_____

The script for my intention: _____

_____

_____

_____

_____

Actions I can take to support my intention: _____

_____

_____

_____

_____

Date _____

I feel alive and free!

Today I am grateful for: _____

_____

_____

_____

My intention is: _____

_____

_____

_____

The script for my intention: _____

_____

_____

_____

Actions I can take to support my intention: _____

_____

_____

_____

Date _____

My dreams of today will be
my reality tomorrow.

....

Today I am grateful for: _____

_____

_____

_____

My intention is: _____

_____

_____

_____

The script for my intention: _____

_____

_____

_____

_____

Actions I can take to support my intention: _____

_____

_____

_____

_____

Date _____

I move forward and never look back.

....

Today I am grateful for: _____

_____

_____

_____

_____

My intention is: _____

_____

_____

_____

_____

The script for my intention: _____

_____

_____

_____

_____

Actions I can take to support my intention: _____

_____

_____

_____

_____

Date _____

I am strong. I am ready. I am enough.

··

Today I am grateful for: _____

_____

_____

_____

My intention is: _____

_____

_____

_____

The script for my intention: _____

_____

_____

_____

Actions I can take to support my intention: _____

_____

_____

_____

Date _____

It's my new day. It's my new life.

....

Today I am grateful for: _____
_____
_____
_____

My intention is: _____
_____
_____
_____

The script for my intention: _____
_____
_____
_____
_____

Actions I can take to support my intention: _____
_____
_____
_____
_____

Date _____

I look at the world as though everyone loves one another.

....

Today I am grateful for: _____

_____

_____

_____

_____

My intention is: _____

_____

_____

_____

The script for my intention: _____

_____

_____

_____

_____

Actions I can take to support my intention: _____

_____

_____

_____

_____

Date _____

I love myself unconditionally.

....

Today I am grateful for: _____

_____

_____

_____

_____

My intention is: _____

_____

_____

_____

The script for my intention: _____

_____

_____

_____

_____

Actions I can take to support my intention: _____

_____

_____

_____

_____

Date _____

My life is full and peaceful.

....

Today I am grateful for: _____

_____

_____

_____

My intention is: _____

_____

.

_____

The script for my intention: _____

_____

_____

_____

Actions I can take to support my intention: _____

_____

_____

_____

Date _____

Today, I choose fierce, limitless bravery.

Today I am grateful for: _____

_____

_____

_____

_____

My intention is: _____

_____

_____

_____

_____

The script for my intention: _____

_____

_____

_____

_____

Actions I can take to support my intention: _____

_____

_____

_____

_____

Date _____

Bring. It. On.

....

Today I am grateful for: _____

_____

_____

_____

_____

My intention is: _____

_____

_____

_____

_____

The script for my intention: _____

_____

_____

_____

_____

_____

Actions I can take to support my intention: _____

_____

_____

_____

_____

I freely give and receive love.

Today I am grateful for: _____

_____

_____

_____

_____

My intention is: _____

_____

_____

_____

The script for my intention: _____

_____

_____

_____

Actions I can take to support my intention: _____

_____

_____

_____

_____

Date _____

I sit in the place of love, for love is the highest of all emotions.

....

Today I am grateful for: _____

_____

_____

_____

_____

My intention is: _____

_____

_____

_____

The script for my intention: _____

_____

_____

_____

_____

Actions I can take to support my intention: _____

_____

_____

_____

_____

Date _____

I accept beauty, love, and other high-vibrational qualities into my life.

··

Today I am grateful for: ··

··

··

··

··

My intention is: ··

··

··

··

The script for my intention: ··

··

··

··

··

Actions I can take to support my intention: ······························

··

··

··

··

"*You are always in a state of creation. You always have been. You are creating your reality in every moment of every day. You are creating your future with every single thought: either consciously or subconsciously. You can't take a break from it and decide not to create because creation never stops. The Law of Attraction never stops working.*"

—JACK CANFIELD

A Final Word

YOU DID IT! YOU FINISHED THIS book! You are now well on your way to manifesting the life you've always dreamed of. I know it sounds kind of crazy to consider, but you *can* and you *will* have a life that far exceeds anything you've imagined. The Law of Attraction and the process of manifestation are all about surrendering your heart to the process, changing your mindset and thought patterns, and inviting in what you want and deserve in life.

Remember, it's all about creating it, living it, and embracing it. When we surrender our hearts and allow ourselves the freedom to invent a life that we are over-the-moon excited about, our vibration and mood rise without us even doing anything!

Imagine the speed at which you will manifest your intentions when you take what you've learned here and apply it to your life, skillfully keeping your thoughts positive and in a heightened state of vibration. Allowing yourself to embrace and accept this new way of being, living, and thinking is the cherry on top.

Never, ever doubt that your dreams can become your reality. The work you do on yourself with the help of this book will stick with you the rest of your life. Congratulations and namaste!

Resources

Ask and It Is Given: Learning to Manifest Your Desires, by Esther and Jerry Hicks (Hay House, 2005)
This is one of my favorite books on the Law of Attraction and manifesting. Esther and Jerry Hicks have written several books on the subject, but this one is their first, and it's just extraordinary.

Insight Timer
Insight Timer is a meditation app with more than 12,000 teachers and 19 million meditators from all over the world where you can find meditations to raise your vibration, discover more about the Law of Attraction and manifesting, and learn about the world's religions, philosophies, and anything you can think of spiritually. I am a meditation teacher on the app, and I would *love* for you to seek me out!

Manifestation Journal for Beginners Empowerment Group
Facebook.com/groups/581107142890952
This Facebook group complements this book and is where we go to share our successes and challenges, ask questions, find gratitude buddies, and so much more! Come on over, and let's navigate these waters together!

The Secret (movie/documentary, 2006)
Executive producer of the film and author of the book by the same title, Rhonda Byrne clarifies the Law of Attraction with expert interviews, illustrations, and references. You will feel your vibration rise as you watch it. This movie, quite literally, changed my life and will do the same for you.

References

Byrne, Rhonda. *The Secret*. New York, NY: Atria Books, 2006.

Easwaran, Eknath. *Bhagavad Gita*. Boulder, CO. Shambhala Publications, 2004.

Encyclopaedia Britannica, eds. "New Thought." *Encyclopaedia Britannica*. Accessed August 27, 2021. Britannica.com/event /New-Thought.

Hay, Louise. "Louise Hay." Accessed August 25, 2021. LouiseHay.com.

Heriot, Drew, dir. *The Secret*. 2006; Melbourne, Australia: Prime Time Productions, 2006. Amazon.com/Secret-Rhonda-Byrne /dp/B00DDOWK5I/ref=sr_1_2?dchild=1&keywords=the+secret &qid=1629924025&s=movies-tv&sr=1-2.

Jim Carrey Instagram fan page (@jimcarreyhere). Accessed August 25, 2021. Instagram.com/jimcarreyhere/.

MMAViral. "Conor McGregor—The Law of Attraction." YouTube video, 10:04. May 29, 2020. YouTube.com/watch?v=9IcqaStL8_Y.

Oprah Winfrey. "What I Know for Sure." Oprah.com. Accessed August 25, 2021. Oprah.com/omagazine/what-oprah-knows -for-sure-get-a-life-lift.

WW. "Oprah's 2020 Vision Tour Visionaries: Jennifer Lopez Interview." YouTube video, 46:03. March 4, 2020. YouTube.com /watch?v=BQOSiqJdPNY.

About the Author

Lauri Albert is an internationally recognized spiritual medium, intuitive, certified meditation teacher with davidji, podcast host, and empowerment coach who connects Spirit with living souls through readings, meditations, and divine healings.

Working in the highest vibration, Lauri utilizes her connection with Spirit to teach others how to tap into their unique spiritual gifts and develop an individualized meditation practice to raise personal vibration. Lauri also leads classes and seminars for individuals on manifesting the life of their dreams. Her daily podcast, *In the Flow with Lauri Albert*, is designed to open minds and hearts through meditation, absolute positivity, and spirituality. Each day, she chats about uplifting subjects and then leads a short meditation to leave the listener confident, happy, and self-assured to begin their day.

Having worked and studied with some of the greatest spiritual teachers of our time, Lauri's goal is to transcend earthly beliefs as well as the boundaries that restrain us from living our lives fully, completely, and magically. Visit her at LauriAlbert.com.

CPSIA information can be obtained
at www.ICGtesting.com
Printed in the USA
JSHW051709220122
22162JS00003B/3

9 781638 073727